GaiaStar Mandalas

ECSTATIC VISIONS OF THE LIVING EARTH

BONNIE BELL AND DAVID TODD

Pomegranate

San Francisco

Dedicated to the memory of two men with great hearts,
William Bell and Ron Berkowitz

Published by Pomegranate Communications, Inc.
Box 6099, Rohnert Park, California 94927
1-800-277-1428; www.pomegranate.com

Pomegranate Europe Ltd.
Fullbridge House, Fullbridge
Maldon, Essex CM9 4LE, England

Library of Congress Cataloging-in-Publication Data
Bell, Bonnie.
    Gaiastar mandalas : ecstatic visions of the living earth / Bonnie Bell, David Todd,
       p. cm.
    ISBN 0-7649-1739-0
    1. Photomontage. 2. Photography—Digital techniques. 3. Mandala in art. I. Todd,
David, 1952–II. Title.

TR685.B4414 2001
 779—dc21

                                                                           2001021763

Pomegranate Catalog No. A609
ISBN 0-7649-1739-0

Cover and interior design by Winslow Colwell, Wind Design, Middlebury, Vermont

Printed in China

10 09 08 07 06 05 04 03 02 01   10 9 8 7 6 5 4 3 2 1

Contents

Introduction

As we crested the drive, we saw it for the first time. Majestic, wreathed in mist, it rose like a granite pyramid from the valley floor. The Rock. Its surrounding lands have been haven to wildlife and indigenous peoples for centuries, and the area is still mostly untouched. Taking up residence within sight of this giant was like moving into an Earth cathedral whose rolling hills and deep arroyos shimmered with spirited beauty. Living here has awakened our outer and inner sight and propelled us to create visionary Nature art.

The visual infusion we received when we moved onto this property has been translated into the many images you see in this book. Every picture starts with real objects from Nature. Most of the objects are from right around our home (in Mendocino County, California). The flowers and plants are wild or growing on our deck. The feathers and wings are medicine gifts from our local birds and butterflies. The colored rocks are from the creek beds and hillsides around us. Certain crystals and exotic feathers have also migrated to this sanctuary, drawn as we were to its wild splendor.

THE ROCKS MADE US DO IT

Arriving at this hilly Eden in 1996 was like coming to a new world. As we explored its environs, our wonder only grew. In our first year here, we hiked through the woods as often as we could, drinking in the details. And while we were honored to make the acquaintance of all the woods' fauna and flora, we were most captivated by the rocks. At first we brought home tiny stones, which were fine examples of the range of mineral colors common to this locale. Soon, though, we made regular forays to the large creek below the Rock in search of new treasures. Like children in a candy store, we would exclaim over every brilliant treat we discovered. Mostly we just admired and photographed these stones, but some volunteered to be part of a special collection on our deck. During the first year, we hauled hundreds of pounds of rocks up the hillsides to place in our growing outdoor shrine.

Earth Rock

One day, walking home from the creek, already laden with stones, we came across an exceptional rock standing along a deer trail. It was typical of a special formation that we had encountered in the area. It was layered like a thick sandwich: the outer edges were dark red, while the inside was a tiger-like pattern of rich yellow swirled with white quartz. This particular piece weighed more than one hundred pounds and had a strong presence. We got the notion to move the rock to a clearing about three hundred feet up the steep slope from where it lay; there it could stand as the center of a stone circle.

We went home and got a handcart and some rope and returned to the rock. With its permission (yes, we communed with the rocks), we loaded it onto the cart. Laughing and dizzy with the effort, we managed to drag the rock up the hillside to its new home. We named it the Earth Rock because its rich red-yellow mass seemed to embody the grounding warmth of our home planet. In the days that followed, we ringed the Earth Rock with a circle of smaller quartz stones. In our next step, we then marked out a five-pointed star within the circle. Contemplating this image of interpenetrating Earth and Star further catalyzed our vision and inspired the name "GaiaStar."

Gaia is an ancient name for Earth as goddess. In recent years it has been used by systems scientists, such as James Lovelock, to refer to the Earth as a planetary whole. According to systems theory, the Earth meets all the criteria for being a self-regulating, living system. On a global scale, it functions much like an animate being. This scientific theory dovetails with a common intuitive response to the Earth as a great (most often feminine) personage. In the Western world, Earth is personified as "Mother Nature."

Creating a ceremonial setting for the Earth Rock solidified our partnership with the planet. In a very real way, all the art in this book has been created by the Earth, with our assistance. Who, after all, compressed the colored minerals into such gorgeous patterns, and who birthed the myriad growing things? We are very grateful for this collaboration with Nature. We see ourselves as trustees of an abundant Gaian treasury.

REMIXING REALITY

Even before moving to Mendocino, we had begun making art as a way of comprehending a major shift in our awareness and experience. Whereas previously we had identified divinity only in the high or cosmic domains, we had begun to contact that spirit within the Earth. This was a somewhat disorienting affair, as we found our old ideas about what is sacred turned on their heads. Since we did not really have a vocabulary for describing this growing awareness, we depicted it in collages.

Collage is a medium eminently suited for this kind of revisioning. It involves juxtaposing visual elements (either images or objects) to create a composite that is novel or surreal. It is all about taking pieces of one thing and grafting them onto something else. Size and perspective are malleable. This was ideal for our exploration.

These collages expressed a central theme: Awareness stretches from the highest to the lowest dimensions; spirit and matter form a continuum of being. The figures in our collages all displayed this transdimensional quality. We had angels with bodies of rock, cats that flew, and roses that spilled gems from their centers. We worked again and again with pictures of the Earth from space. At first, we put a halo around the globe, then gave her a crown, and eventually wings. Certain elements were repeated and gained special meaning for us. We were developing an iconographic language, or visual shorthand. The images conveyed our sense of the continuous and sacred "livingness" that reached from below to above.

We began to understand our artwork as a kind of visual alchemy. In traditional alchemy, minerals were cooked together until their elements split apart. Thus dissolved, they could recombine into a new and precious substance. Like alchemists liberating gold from lead, we remixed pictorial elements in order to unveil the bright potential within ourselves and our material world.

In the year before we moved to Mendocino, the source material for these images began to change. Whereas our earliest collages were mostly composed of clippings from magazines, we now started to incorporate photographic elements from our home and our nature walks. The images became less abstract and more personal. Our statues, our cat, the trees in our yard became part of the pictures. By the time we arrived at our new home, we had

SeedSong Empowerment

eight or nine such pieces. In the months that followed, we created more than a dozen others, prominently featuring elements from our hillside retreat. We created these pieces originally for our own use, never thinking of sharing them more widely. They were our way of modeling an upgraded existence.

INTO THE HEART OF MATTER

With every month, our partnership with Nature continued to deepen. We were—and are—unabashedly in love with the multihued world. We started taking more close-up photographs, filling whole frames with the neon green of moss, the scarlet of manzanita bark, and the rainbow surfaces of the rocks in the creek.

In the fall of our second year here, we started a new collage, using a close-up photograph of the Earth Rock as its background. In order to get a full visual field, we used two prints of the same photograph of the rock; we rotated the prints so that they came together as a reverse image. Something was triggered by putting these twin photographs together. Shortly after doing that, we bought a digital scanner and began experimenting with our close-up photographs.

We scanned a number of photographs and worked with them using Adobe's Photoshop software. When we first took a section of a photograph

Ecstasy (detail)

and flipped it to form a symmetry, we made an electrifying discovery: at the intersections between the two identical parts, all sorts of creatures and objects appeared. The doubling of the image opened a visual portal through which we could see a whole new world within our world.

To say that we dived deep into making these symmetries does not begin to describe our passion. We spent hours creating and then examining these pictures. We started with some of our favorite rock photographs. In one of the first such pictures a figure appeared that astonished us. In a symmetry made from the rock we called Swirl Rock, the complete figure of an angel appeared. This confirmed that we were onto something good, so we made more images. Looking at these images really turned us on. It was more than just the fun of seeing some wild yet recognizable face pop out of the art. We started to feel an integrative effect, as if the higher aspects of ourselves had found their reflection in the material world.

Seeing these figures appear in so-called inert rock was a classic "through the looking glass" moment. It was a vision of the infinitely rich interior life of matter. The mirroring of an image allowed our brains to connect with something that our bodies already knew: The microcosmic world

Swirl Rock

Angel in Swirl Rock

is as complex and inhabited as the human and cosmic domains. We are, the planet is, alive inside. Cells, molecules, and atoms dance in a vast quantum sea. By multiplying and rearranging the patterning information from a photograph, we had opened a visionary doorway into Nature's core.

Over the months that followed, we evolved the symmetrical artforms and began sharing them with others. Up to that point, we had seen our art only as a tool for our own personal transformation, and as our way of invoking a new reality. But our friends said the art had a euphoric effect on them as well. People began asking to take the pieces home to use for meditation or simply to enjoy their natural beauty. Everyone said they felt drawn into the images, and they really liked where that took them.

The Full Circle

We quickly expanded beyond our rock photographs to make symmetries from other visual materials, such as flowers and feathers. Each image that emerged from these highly textured and colored objects had its own vibrant effect. Part of what was so stunning was seeing the natural geometries arise when we assembled these images. One such picture we called The Full Circle. It was made from a very quartz-filled section of our friend, the Earth Rock. When we chose the photographic section to work with, we were not trying to create a circle, but when the pieces were assembled, a full circle emerged in the patterning itself.

The appearance of this circle impressed us. It spoke of

the inherent power in these natural images. We began to call these pictures "Matter Mandalas." Mandalas are a form of Hindu sacred art that also have been highly developed within the Buddhist tradition. Mandalas are usually based on a circular shape, depicting a sphere or chalice of positive energies. The balanced patterns and geometric shapes that appeared in our images, although not always circular, could be compared to those in classic mandalas. And, like traditional sacred art, our art had an elevating effect on people. It was a spontaneous modern expression of the blessing energy that is conveyed in traditional mandala art.

We emphasize the spontaneity of this process, because that is what spurred us on. The emergence of these mandalas had more the quality of revelation than design. And yet, our own visionary intention was clearly part of the mix. We had asked for a way to transmit the graceful potency we felt in our communion with the Earth. It seemed we had found our means in this style of art.

Neither of us had any training or prior experience as artists. We had previously worked with the written and spoken word, via editing, writing, and public speaking. Although we had always been inspired by traditional sacred art, especially from the Hindu and Buddhist traditions, we never imagined ourselves creating it. However, beginning with our early collages and accelerating with the revelation of the Matter Mandalas, we found ourselves increasingly focused in a visual medium.

Telling our story in this linear fashion makes the process sound rather orderly, when it wasn't. We were more like Alice after having drunk from the bottle: We were getting bigger whether we liked it or not. In retrospect, we refer to this process as "going Gaian." It is the exhilarating—and sometimes disconcerting—process of awakening to wide-bandwidth existence. We retrained our attention and tuned into levels of sensory input that we had not previously been able to access.

We began this visionary adventure as fairly rational, if idealistic, people. For

Go-Ma

decipher a message in one language and encode it into another. We had the experience of making contact at a core level with our planet and finding it full of spirit-light and presence. Our immediate mission was to find a way to "notate," in the form of visual (i.e., photographic) information, the vibrational essences we drew from that contact. When we selected a portion of a photograph, it became a bit of source code that we reassembled into mandala images. The images could then speak in the Earth's visual voice about the emergence of a new global possibility.

many years we had assumed major responsibilities in international nonprofit and for-profit businesses. We had been seriously applied to the exploration of consciousness. Now we found ourselves engaged in an equally rigorous and ecstatic process of scanning and remixing bits of visual information. We were a little like Richard Dreyfuss in the movie *Close Encounters of the Third Kind*, who sculpted his mashed potatoes into a dream-seen mountain. Our art emerged from a trancelike state of perceptual openness. Through a process of reception and distillation, we discovered a visual vocabulary that could then begin to convey our experience of the living planet.

We thought of ourselves as translators, people who

After creating many Matter Mandalas, we began using these geometrical patterns as backgrounds and borders for our collage figures. We created an initial series of ten figures, who we thought of as "transdimensional Allies." The original characters contained elements from many of the world's traditions (the wings of Isis, a Tibetan crown, a Huichol Indian mask). They also had parts that were earthy (mushroom wings, a body of stone). Some of the later figures literally emerged from the Matter Mandalas, in that they are figures who came into being through one of the symmetries. (An example is Go-Ma, above, who came from the image titled Rock Mother, on page 83.)

Each Ally figure was featured in its own setting, or doorway, made from our mandala patterns. Soon the ten figures became a clan of twenty-one, and we saw that, by devising a complementary sequence of Matter Mandalas, we could create an entire series of diverse images. This series depicted a futuristic story of planetary evolution. In these images we summarized our experience of our home environment as a "turned-on world," a place where spirit and matter happily interpenetrate. We called this series *The GaiaStar Codex*.

The sixty-four images that comprise *The GaiaStar Codex* form a basic "pictogrammar" of our visual language. We worked with five basic elements: rocks, plants, feathers/wings, flowers, and crystals. These elements were analogous to the five traditional alchemical elements: earth, water, air, fire, and ether. Five elements were enough, it seemed, to build a visual world. We wanted these images to be used actively, in the form of a card deck or interactive system. After the pictures were completed, we named them, wrote commentaries, and devised many ways the Codex images could be used for self-empowerment and to access guidance. With the help of Pomegranate Communications, we published the entire series and system as *The GaiaStar Codex: Seeds of a Turned-On World*.

> ... an emerging global being is forming in our midst. This Gaian entity contains countless diverse species and life-forms. Just as differentiated cells organize to form a complex body, myriad individual aspects of Gaia are coalescing into a new kind of planetary unity. This is happening electronically through the worldwide computer web, but it is also happening at profound levels of biological and spiritual identity. The global being is taking shape where grand laws of self-organization intersect with a planetwide intention to make a quantum leap.

> From this fertile conjunction, a familiar yet uplifted Earth emerges: luminous, self-aware, awake as many-in-one. This is a turned-on world—the GaiaStar. (*The GaiaStar Codex*, p. 6)

Even while completing *The GaiaStar Codex* we developed more forms of mandala art. One style, which we called Healing Mandalas, was based on a twelve-sided wheel or star. Both the precisely circular shape and the twelve-part structure seemed to be suited to communicating healing energy. Again using the five elements of rocks, plants, wings, flowers, and crystals, we created a series of thirty-five Healing Mandalas to be used singly or arranged together in a "array." We called the whole series "The Splendor Array." Our desire to share the restorative energies of the Earth through this "medicine art" was very warmly received. The full potential of these images, now being used in hospitals and healing centers, is still unfolding.

Like parent plants seeding new growth, these first two series have sprouted many new forms. Each form has its own geometric and elemental integrity, and each is invested with its own uplifting intention, but they all share an underlying vibration: Earth Ecstasy. This is our name for the charged energy that flows from the wholehearted embrace between spirit and matter. Earth Ecstasy is the juicy glow that radiates from the images. It can be enjoyed for its own sake or used for self-healing and expanding awareness. Our job as artists is to create diverse visual vessels to convey this never-ending flow.

No description of how this art evolved would be complete without acknowledging how we use guidance in its creation. We each listen to our deepest intuition in determining how any given piece should take shape. Often, one of us will get an initial holistic vision of the image as well as some idea of which elements should be used. We create a first version and then remix the piece, yet still following our core intuition, until it comes together in a way that makes us both say "Yes."

TECHNO-SACRED VISIONS

Art alters us. This certainty underlies the initiatory and healing imagery of all human cultures. Our artist-ancestors who painted stirring visions on cave walls knew intuitively what modern science now verifies: We Homo sapiens are greatly affected, as most creatures are, by the color/shape/figure input we receive from the outside world. As a matter of survival and also evolutionary adaptation, we are structured to respond (amid many simultaneous sensory responses) to the vibrational wave-pattern information we take in through our optical sensors.

Our inborn visual response mechanisms, although clearly geared to survival purposes, can also be directed toward lofty goals. Sacred scientists in every age have, via meditative and altered states, envisioned how to use art for the purposes of consciousness-expansion and healing. Through a process of deep self-informing and trance vision, these men and women created imagery designed to induce changes of state. In doing this work, the artist-priests tapped into a reservoir of sight-triggered responses to help induce a desired end. Although some sacred art is representational, depicting divine beings or totems, much is abstract and geometrical in nature.

Cultures all around the world have worked with stylized sacred images. In the Americas, we find medicine art in the form of geometric sand paintings and other ceremonial symbols. Islamic art abounds with sacred diagrams, as do the European alchemical arts. The cosmological charts of the Mayan and Jain religions are exquisitely detailed. The list could go on and on. Wherever people are engaged in ritual practice, such artforms evolve. Via the wavelengths of their colors and the numerical messages embedded in their geometries, they stimulate our brains and nervous systems in observable ways. Especially when augmented with other sensory triggers, such as scent and sound, these artforms can activate new capabilities and awareness.

Mandalas, originally from India, have migrated to many new lands. Combining a central geometric enclosure with a whole variety of additional symbols and figures, they can transmit information on many levels. GaiaStar Mandalas likewise convey a wealth of transformational input.

What distinguishes our images from other mandalas is both the method of their creation and their core purpose. Classic mandalas are related to a specific belief system. Their purpose is to provide significant visual-vibratory support for practitioners of a given tradition. GaiaStar Mandalas, however, are not aligned with any specific religion or practice. Although archetypal shapes and symbols from many faiths appear spontaneously when we reorder the photographic source materials, GaiaStar Mandalas are tradition-free. They speak in a universal voice.

Classic mandalas are also created by hand according to very specific geometries and color schemes. You could say that traditional mandalas are composed with "analog" (realistic) elements via analog technology (painting or drawing). Our GaiaStar Mandalas take shape when we remix analog source materials (the rocks, flowers, and so on) via digital technology. When the raw materials of Gaia are thus digitized and rearranged, they gain a new kind of power. In the digital context, a potent meeting takes place. Chaos, in the form of the fractal patterning of Nature, melds with Order, in the form of the intentional geometries we create via software. This marriage yields endlessly fascinating combinations of human-made as well as Earth-made patterns. This process is part of the thrill we achieve in creating these images. We are never quite sure of what we will see until all the pieces come together.

SOUND TRACKS FOR THE EYES

In *The GaiaStar Codex*, we call our images "songs clothed in light." This description points to the vibrational fullness of GaiaStar Mandalas. In arranging the images in this book, we chose to mix the various styles of mandalas rather than group them by category. Each section is like a track on a CD, sequenced for your viewing pleasure. This arrangement encourages the eyes and mind to move around, to focus in and out at different depths, and to take in the various "notes" in the images. Each of the six sections has a "song" title, reflecting the theme that plays through the selected mandalas. In the end, though, all the images are variations on the grand theme of Earth Ecstasy.

The main admonition in looking at these images is to enjoy them. As medicine art, they evoke delight and uplift. They are a way of taking in the richness of the Earth. The only technique we recommend is to feel them as much as see them. The images communicate on many levels. One time, you may notice the geometries and the ways the shapes interact. Another time, you may focus immediately on the fabulous creatures that pop out of the images. You may perceive certain pictures more in terms of energy or waves of emotion. Every time you look at the same picture, you may see or experience different things. Feel free to experiment. These images extend an open invitation to explore Earth's visual domains.

Those who wish to use the mandalas for meditative purposes will find them easy to approach. Pick an image that really speaks to you. Find a way to hold or set the image so that you can look at it without tensing your body. Then simply gaze at the chosen picture. You will be led by your eyes and feeling into the visionary space that we call the GaiaStar. You can go as deeply as you choose and receive as much as you like. If you find your eyes wanting to close, let them do so. You can still feel the energy of the image and see it in your mind's eye. (For free-standing mounted prints of GaiaStar images ideal for meditation, see page III.)

People report many effects from meditating on these mandalas: some experience bliss states; some gain new information; others find the contemplation restful and healing. There are those who actually "hear" music in the mandalas, and others who find them reappearing in dreams. Every person responds uniquely to these visions. What people report most consistently is that this art helps them see the Earth with new eyes, giving them heightened awareness of her illumined nature.

Here is our testimony as makers and users of these mandalas: Gaia has tremendous beauty-power, which she freely shares through these visions. We were called to create this art so that many people could access her treasuries. Through these images, you can interface with and feast on the lit-up energy within Earth. May this bring you and our planet great blessings.

Bonnie Bell, February, 2001

Note to the Reader

Below each picture you will find its title followed by the source material from which the image was made. When the objects have common names, such as "star-gazer lily" or "oak leaves," we listed them. To distinguish rocks from each other, we gave them descriptive names, for example, "red-green rock" or "swirl rock."

In some of the images you will notice rays of light and neon highlights. These effects occur when we put the objects themselves (not just a photograph) directly on the scanner. The laser lights of the scanner refract in the surfaces and features of the objects. This effect happens most dramatically with the crystals. See LumiMatter, page 97, for an example of this effect. The quartz crystal used in this image is completely clear and colorless; the bright colors you see result from refracted light.

The word "cyberdelic" precedes a few of the source materials (for instance, "cyberdelic turkey feathers"). This term means that we used software to shift the original color of the object. Unless specifically noted as cyberdelic, the colors you see in each image came entirely from the natural objects as captured by the scanner.

Go
Gaian

15

I Rise [Iris petals]

Dimensity [Tiger rock]

Humor Us [Broadway rose]

Potency [Milk thistle]

Healing Mandala #28   [Rose]

Earth Ecstasy [Orchid and parrot feathers]

Healing Mandala #14 [Ivy]

Input [Fluorite, pyrite, and redwood]

Play [Iris]

Full Circle [Earth rock]

Melding [Pheasant and macaw feathers]

Unity [Neptune rock]

Kindred Spirits [Flicker and parrot feathers]

Inner Light [Fluorite pyramid]

Activation [Neptune rock]

A Grand Convergence

Trust [Brown butterfly]

Vision [Gloria rock and cyberdelic rose]

Vivid Dreams [Hydrangea petals]

TerraSolis [Chrysocolla and cyberdelic quartz cluster]

Healing Mandala #2 [Jupiter rock]

Wisdom [Madrone wood]

Harmonics [All cyberdelic: rock, fungus, crystal, petals, and feathers]

Healing Mandala #23 [Orchids]

Gleam [Oak leaves]

Elixir [Prayer plant]

Take Heart [Iris petals]

Integration [Cyberdelic turkey feathers and clear crystal]

Tonic [Cyberdelic prayer plant]

Healing Mandala #19 [Peacock feathers]

CenterPeace [Rose petal mix]

Where
Infinity
Meets
Reality

47

Healing Mandala #30 [Mixed stones]

LumiNexus [Crystal, orchid, cyberdelic hawk feather, and rock]

Yes [Mixed petals]

Imagination [Geranium and crepe myrtle]

Healing Mandala #9 [Oak leaves]

Healing Mandala #17 [Cyberdelic woodpecker feathers]

Amazement [Rose petal mix]

Healing Mandala #22 [Mixed petals]

Completion [Fluorite, macaw feathers, and marigold]

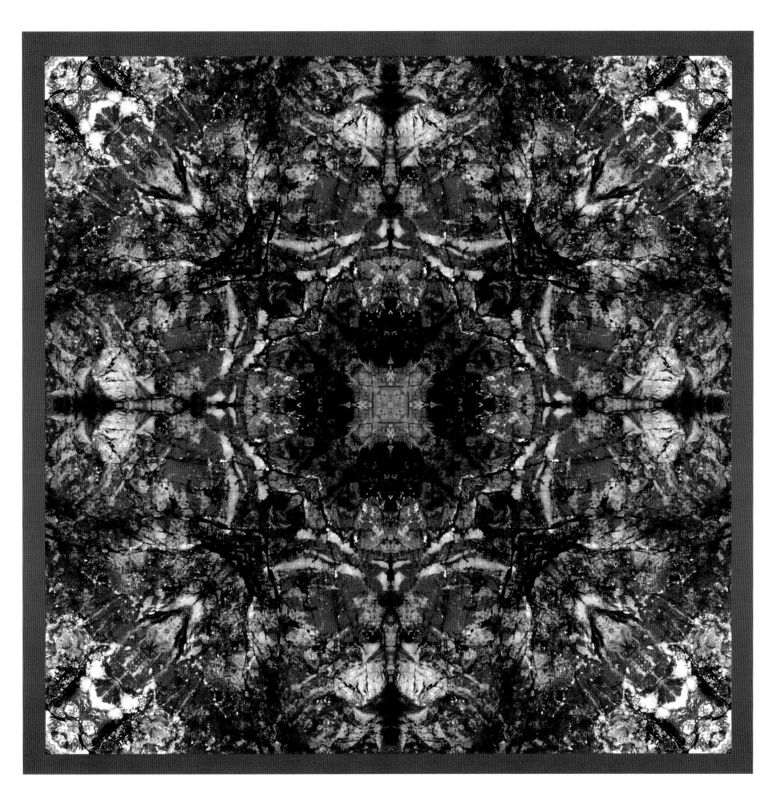

Reality [Red-green rock]

Cohere [Owl feathers]

Abundance [Mixed petals]

Vitality [Madrone leaf]

Delight [Oak leaf]

Myth [Mushroom]

Sublime
Alchemy

Ecstasy [Mixed petals]

OmniBeing [Madrone wood]

MetaFission [Red-white rock]

Incarnation [Gloria rock]

Presence [Swirl rock]

Euphoria [Moon rock]

Vortex [Crocus]

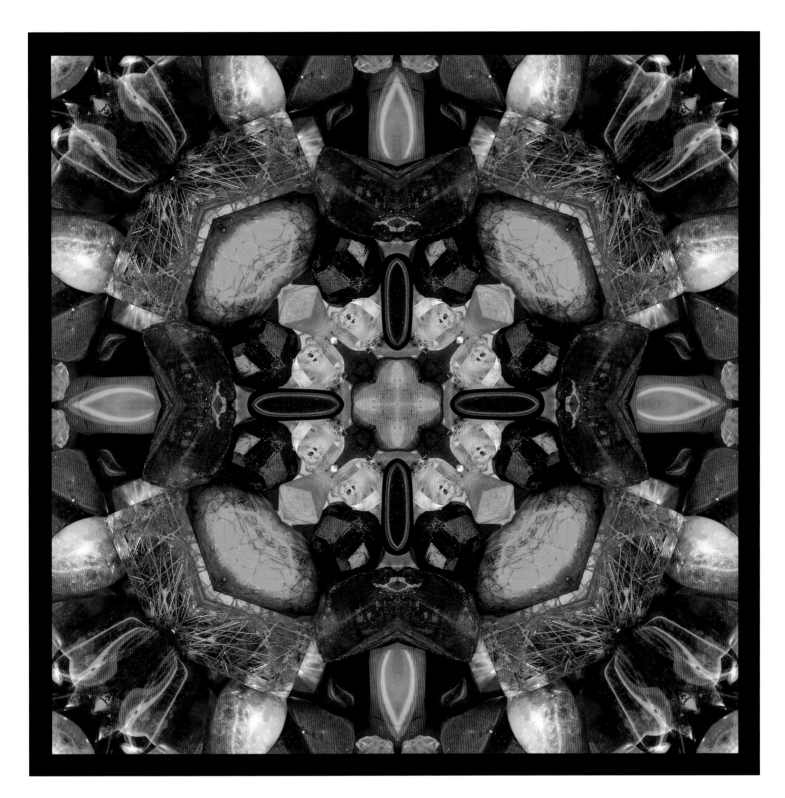

Brilliance [Mixed stones]

Healing Mandala #20 [Cyberdelic butterfly]

Tribe [Orchid and crystal ball]

Mystery [Cyberdelic rose]

Desire [Uranus rock and sage leaf]

Resonance [Parrot feathers]

Healing Mandala #34 [Fluorite]

Healing Mandala #21 [Eagle feather]

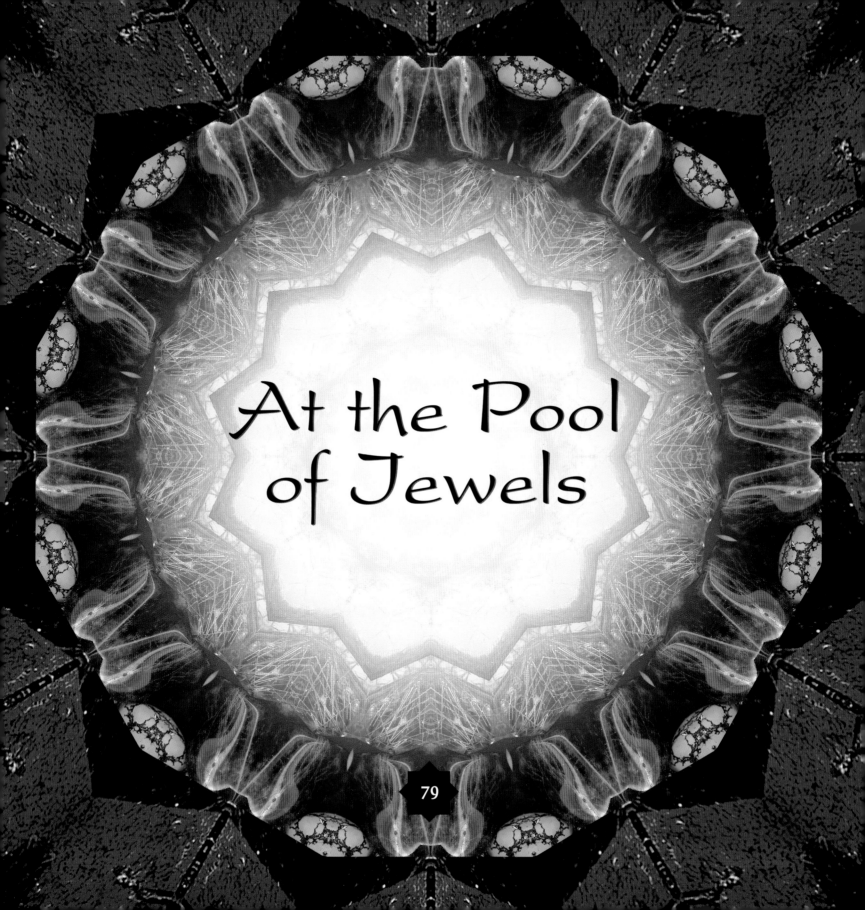

At the Pool
of Jewels

Passion [Rose]

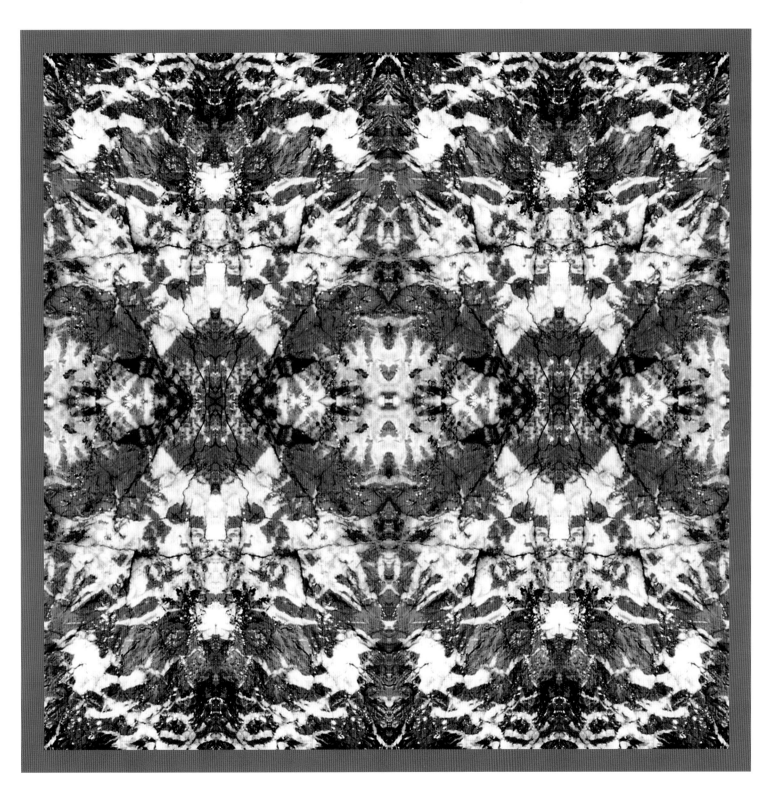

Sentience [Earth rock]

Transparency [Clear crystal]

Rock Mother [Orange-teal rock]

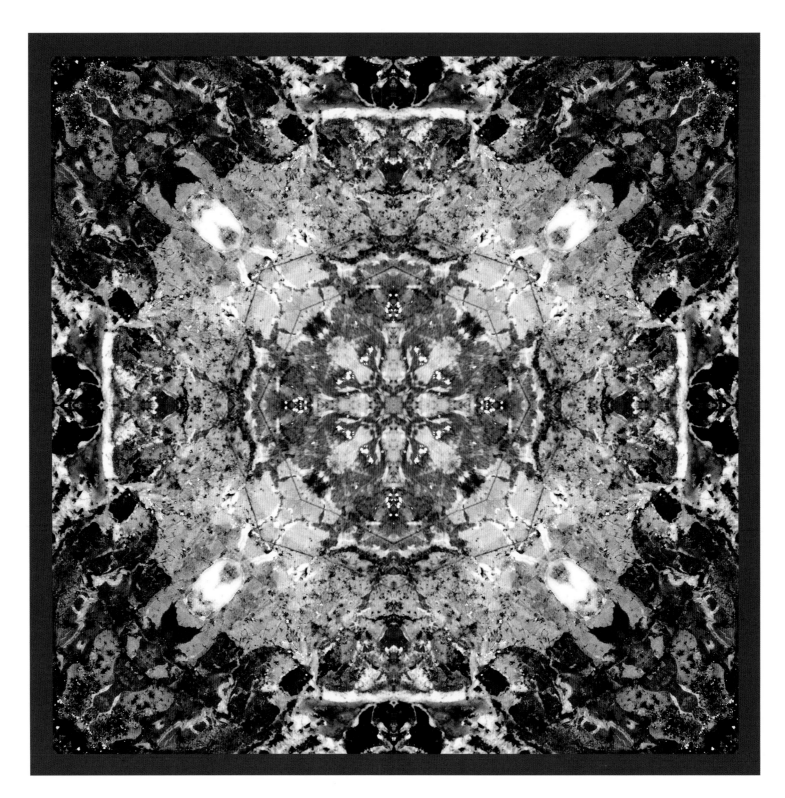

Sacred Space [Uranus rock]

Healing Mandala #18 [Cyberdelic turkey feathers]

Healing Mandala #35 [Mixed stones]

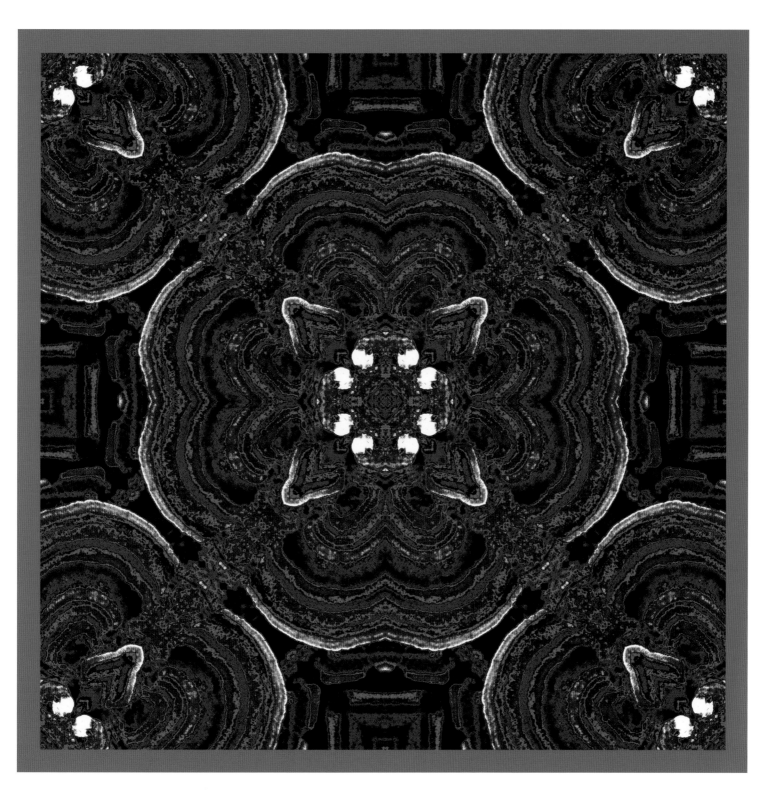

Feel Good [Cyberdelic tree fungus]

Fusion [Fluorite and cyberdelic turkey feathers]

Energy [Neptune rock]

Cool [Woodpecker feathers]

Healing Mandala #13 [Prayer leaf]

Healing Mandala #4 [Uranus rock]

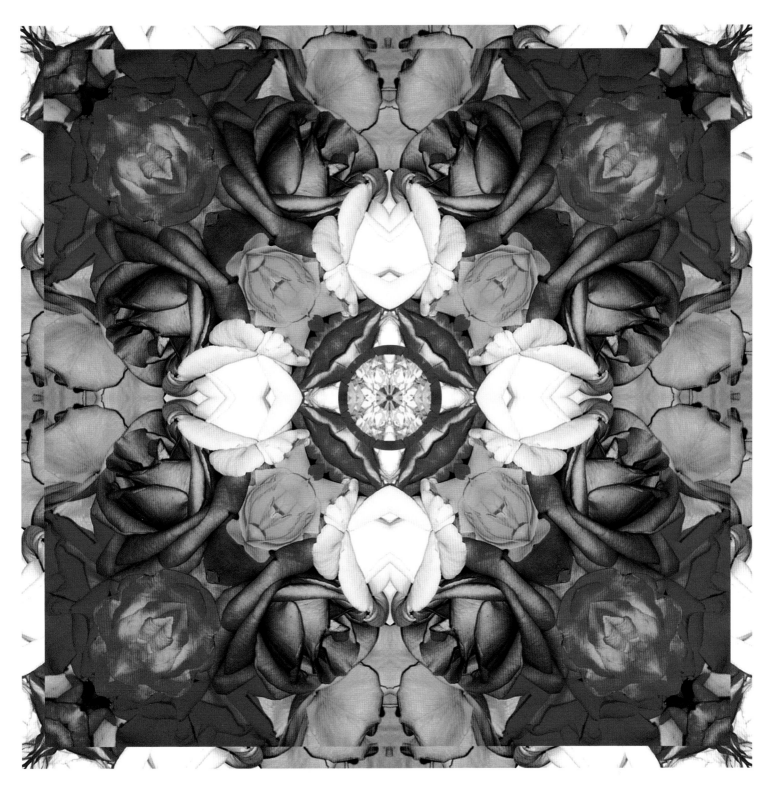

Family Jewels [Diamond and roses]

Glory [Mixed stones]

Love Wins

95

Gaian Arc [Rainbow, chrysocolla, and mixed petals]

LumiMatter [Clear crystal]

ReCreation [Pansies and lantana]

Get Down [Tribal rock]

Ring of Fire [Marigold petals]

Compassion [Ivy and pheasant feathers]

Healing Mandala #25 [Star-gazer lily]

CosmoSphere [Chrysocolla and cyberdelic: rocks, butterfly, crystal]

Solar Flare [Cyberdelic quartz cluster]

Healing Mandala #16 [Brown butterfly]

Healing Mandala #3 [Blue-gold rock]

Lavender Lamb [Lamb's ear and lavender]

Celebration [Mixed petals and herbs]

Splendor [Geranium and impatiens]

Good Fortune [Uranus rock and peacock feathers]

Visit GaiaStarWorld Online

To explore the lit-up world of the GaiaStar, visit our website

www.GaiaStarWorld.com

where you will find:

★ Fine Art Prints—Select a mandala to use for decoration
or meditation. These high-resolution images are printed
with archival inks on watercolor paper. Mounted and
matted in several sizes for easy framing.

★ Other GaiaStar Arts—Connect with the scents, sounds,
and other media that convey Earth Ecstasy.

★ Education and Services—Learn about using GaiaStar
creations for self-empowerment and transformation.

All services and products can be accessed at
www.GaiaStarWorld.com
or by writing to
GaiaStar, P.O. Box 1385, Ukiah, CA 95482-1385